TAKING A STAND

PARKLAND STUDENTS
CHALLENGE THE NATIONAL RIFLE ASSOCIATION

by Rebecca Rowell

FOCUS READERS

www.focusreaders.com

Copyright © 2019 by Focus Readers, Lake Elmo, MN 55042. All rights reserved. No part of this book may be reproduced or utilized in any form or by any means without written permission from the publisher.

Focus Readers is distributed by North Star Editions:
sales@northstareditions.com | 888-417-0195

Produced for Focus Readers by Red Line Editorial.

Content Consultant: Julie Webber, Professor of Politics & Government, Illinois State University

Photographs ©: Olivier Douliery/Abaca Press/Sipa/AP Images, cover, 1, 25, 39; Joseph Sohm/ Shutterstock Images, 4–5; Rena Schild/Shutterstock Images, 7; Eric Gay/AP Images, 8–9; Red Line Editorial, 10, 21; Janos Rautonen/Shutterstock Images, 13; Ben Moffat/ZUMA Wire/Alamy, 15; jodiecoston/iStockphoto, 16–17; contrastaddict/iStockphoto, 19; KMH Photovideo/Shutterstock Images, 22–23; Sun-Sentinel/ZUMA Wire/Alamy, 26; Michael Nigro/Alamy Live News/Pacific Press/Alamy, 29; Christopher Halloran/Shutterstock Images, 30–31; Mark Van Scyoc/Shutterstock Images, 33; Nicole S Glass/Shutterstock Images, 34; Sheila Fitzgerald/Shutterstock Images, 36–37; Michael Melia/AP Images, 40; Hayk_Shalunts/Shutterstock Images, 42–43; Crush Rush/Shutterstock Images, 45

Library of Congress Cataloging-in-Publication Data
Library of Congress Cataloging-in-Publication Data is available on the Library of Congress website.

ISBN
978-1-64185-357-6 (hardcover)
978-1-64185-415-3 (paperback)
978-1-64185-531-0 (ebook pdf)
978-1-64185-473-3 (hosted ebook)

Printed in the United States of America
Mankato, MN
October, 2018

ABOUT THE AUTHOR

Rebecca Rowell has put her degree in publishing and writing to work as an editor and an author of many books. Recent topics as author include Emmanuel Macron, Xi Jinping, and the American middle class. She lives in Minneapolis, Minnesota.

TABLE OF CONTENTS

CHAPTER 1

MARCH FOR OUR LIVES

On March 24, 2018, students from Marjory Stoneman Douglas High School gathered in Washington, DC. The students were not on a field trip. They were in the nation's capital to speak out against gun violence.

The students were survivors of a school shooting in Parkland, Florida. The month before, a young man had entered their school and started shooting. He had killed 17 people.

Thousands of people gather in Washington, DC, for the March for Our Lives protest.

The students who survived were **traumatized**. They were sad and outraged. The shooting in Parkland was far from the first in the United States. Over the years, many people have asked politicians to create new gun laws. These activists want to make it more difficult to obtain a gun. But change has been slow to come. A major barrier to change is the National Rifle Association (NRA). This powerful organization is against gun control. It **lobbies** in support of gun rights. The NRA has nearly five million members. It also has support from many politicians. Even so, the Parkland students chose to stand up to the NRA.

After the shooting, the survivors quickly started organizing for their cause. In a few weeks, they planned the March for Our Lives protest. On March 24, hundreds of thousands of people attended the event in Washington, DC. Protesters

▲ Students lie in front of the White House in a protest for gun control.

included students, parents, and teachers. Other protesters marched in cities across the country.

At the event in Washington, DC, Parkland students made speeches. Popular singers performed. Other students spoke, too. One was Yolanda Renee King, the nine-year-old granddaughter of Martin Luther King Jr. The speakers varied in age but were united in their message. They had had enough of gun violence and were ready to fight for new gun laws.

CHAPTER 2

MASS SHOOTINGS IN THE UNITED STATES

Mass shootings are not a new problem in the United States. But they have become more frequent in recent decades. They have also become deadlier. Between 2000 and 2017, the death rate per mass shooting nearly tripled.

Definitions of mass shootings vary. According to a 2015 report, a mass shooting involves the murder of four or more people. The victims of the shooting are killed by firearm in a public place.

Roses were placed at Columbine High School to remember the victims of the 1999 shooting.

The report recorded 66 mass shootings between 1999 and 2013. Almost 11 percent of them happened in schools. However, not all school shootings are mass shootings. There are also school shootings with fewer than four victims.

One of the deadliest school shootings in US history took place at Columbine High School.

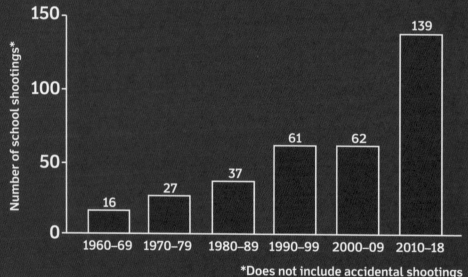

➤ SCHOOL SHOOTINGS ON THE RISE (1960–2018)

Number of school shootings*

Decade	Number
1960–69	16
1970–79	27
1980–89	37
1990–99	61
2000–09	62
2010–18	139

*Does not include accidental shootings

In 1999, two students at the Colorado school killed 13 people. The incident shocked the nation.

Since Columbine, school shootings have taken dozens of lives. Some victims have been young children. In 2012, a man entered Sandy Hook Elementary School in Connecticut. He killed 26 people. Twenty victims were first graders.

The shootings at Columbine and Sandy Hook drew national attention. After Columbine, many schools worked to improve security. They put in metal detectors and cameras. Schools also taught students how to respond to a shooting situation. They began holding monthly drills for practice.

THINK ABOUT IT ◀

Why do you think school shootings have become more frequent?

After Sandy Hook, several states passed new gun laws. Within five years, 210 laws had been enacted to promote gun safety.

Despite these changes, mass shootings continued. Some shootings occurred in places other than schools. In 2017, a man fired into a crowd at a music festival in Las Vegas, Nevada. He killed 59 people and injured more than 500.

The Parkland shooting took place a few months later. On February 14, 2018, a young man walked into Marjory Stoneman Douglas High School with an AR-15 rifle. The 19-year-old gunman had been a student at the school. He walked floor to floor. He shot at people in hallways and classrooms. The shooter's last target was the teachers' lounge on the third floor. Then he dropped his gun and exited the building. He had been in the school for only six minutes. In that time, he killed 17 people.

A banner at Marjory Stoneman Douglas High School honors the victims of the Parkland shooting.

The Parkland shooting brought gun control back to the news. And this time, student survivors were demanding change. After recent school shootings, several states had taken action to pass stricter gun laws. But federal lawmakers were less active. On the federal level, the government had not passed any new gun laws. This lack of change was in part due to the power of the NRA.

ALFONSO CALDERON

One week after the Parkland shooting, a group of survivors visited Florida's state capitol. There, the students spoke out against gun violence. Alfonso Calderon was one of the students who protested.

During a televised interview, Alfonso talked about the shooting. "I was in a closet, locked for four hours with people who I would consider almost family, crying and weeping on me, begging for their lives," Alfonso remembered. He urged others to listen to what the students had to say. They might be young, he explained, but they shouldn't be ignored. "We will not be silenced," Alfonso said. "It has gone on long enough. Just because we are kids, we are not allowed to understand. But, trust me, I understand."

After the shooting, some gun supporters criticized the student activists. But Alfonso stood up for the Parkland survivors. "I understand

▲ Parkland student Alfonso Calderon speaks at a rally against gun violence in April 2018.

what it's like to fear for your life," he said in the interview. "And I don't think we should ever be discredited because of that. I don't think we should ever be silenced because we are just children."

Nina Agrawal and Jaweed Kaleem. "These Are the Florida Students Behind the Movement to End Gun Violence." *LA Times*. LA Times, 23 Feb. 2018. Web. 03 Sept. 2018.

CHAPTER 3

GUNS IN THE UNITED STATES

For guidance on the topic of gun control, US courts look to the Second Amendment to the Constitution. This amendment addresses gun rights. It says a **militia** is "necessary to the security of a free State." Because of that, it says citizens have a right "to keep and bear Arms."

The Second Amendment was **ratified** in 1791 as part of the Bill of Rights. The Revolutionary War (1775–1783) had ended less than a decade before.

Many Americans disagree on the meaning of the Second Amendment.

During the war, American colonists formed militias to fight British soldiers. After winning the war, Americans wanted to protect their new independence. They feared the US government might gain too much power. It might raise a central army to control citizens like the British had done. Under the Second Amendment, state militias could arm themselves against this threat.

Today, some people take the history of the amendment into consideration. They think the Second Amendment gives Americans the right to bear arms only as part of militias. But other

➤ THINK ABOUT IT

What do you think the Second Amendment's creators meant when they wrote it? Do you think the words have a different meaning today? Why or why not?

▲ The AR-15 is a popular rifle in the United States. People use it for hunting and target practice.

people disagree. They think the amendment also gives individuals the right to own guns.

People also debate the use of the word *arms*. Guns today are more powerful than they were in the 1700s. Some people argue that the Second Amendment only applies to guns that were available at that time. Today, mass shooters often use semi-automatic rifles such as the AR-15. A semi-automatic gun reloads automatically. It can also have a high-capacity **magazine**. Guns with high-capacity magazines can fire several bullets in quick succession.

Many Americans want to ban guns that are typically used in mass shootings. In a 2017 survey, 60 percent of Americans wanted stricter laws on the sale of guns. And 48 percent wanted to ban the types of semi-automatic guns often used in mass shootings.

The NRA plays a major role in the gun debate. The organization was created in 1871. The NRA's founders had been Union leaders in the US Civil War (1861–1865). They wanted to improve their troops' shooting skills. But over time, the NRA expanded its focus. The group started training hunters and police officers. It also began taking political action.

In 1976, the NRA created the Political Victory Fund. Through the fund, the NRA donates money to political campaigns. The NRA does this to gain politicians' support. It expects these politicians to support gun rights if they are elected. For example, the NRA donated more than $30 million to Donald Trump's 2016 presidential campaign. With its millions of members and big bank account, the NRA has significant political power.

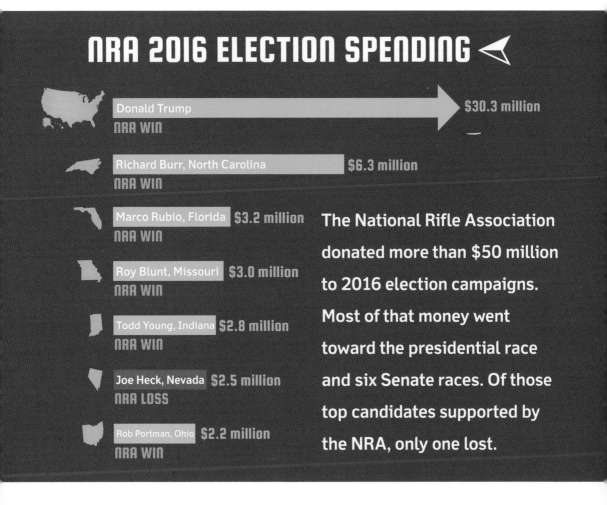

NRA 2016 ELECTION SPENDING

Donald Trump
NRA WIN — $30.3 million

Richard Burr, North Carolina
NRA WIN — $6.3 million

Marco Rubio, Florida — $3.2 million
NRA WIN

Roy Blunt, Missouri — $3.0 million
NRA WIN

Todd Young, Indiana — $2.8 million
NRA WIN

Joe Heck, Nevada — $2.5 million
NRA LOSS

Rob Portman, Ohio — $2.2 million
NRA WIN

The National Rifle Association donated more than $50 million to 2016 election campaigns. Most of that money went toward the presidential race and six Senate races. Of those top candidates supported by the NRA, only one lost.

CHAPTER 4

STUDENTS TAKE A STAND

The Parkland students couldn't undo what had happened to them. But they could try to prevent future mass shootings. The students' actions became known as the Never Again movement. On Twitter, the teen activists spread their message with the hashtag #NeverAgain.

Shortly after the shooting, student Cameron Kasky began raising money on a fundraising website. He raised more than $3.5 million.

Students protest at a Never Again rally in Tallahassee, Florida, in February 2018.

Some of the money went toward organizing the march in Washington, DC. And half of it went to families affected by the shooting.

On February 17, Parkland students protested in Fort Lauderdale, Florida. Emma Gonzalez, a senior at the high school, was one of the speakers. In her speech, Emma read a tweet by President Trump. He had tweeted about the Parkland shooting. Trump said people needed to report those who were "mentally disturbed." He thought this type of action could help prevent mass shootings. Emma said the issue of mass shootings was about more than mental health. It was also about guns. If the shooter had used a knife, Emma explained, he wouldn't have hurt as many people.

After the first protest, 100 Parkland students went to the state capitol in Tallahassee. There, the students urged lawmakers to change Florida's

Parkland student Emma Gonzalez speaks out against gun violence in Washington, DC, on March 24, 2018.

gun laws. They wanted to make it harder to buy semi-automatic guns. They also wanted more thorough **background checks** on gun buyers. Senior Jose Iglesias explained that the students did not want to ban guns. Rather, they wanted stricter laws on buying and selling the most dangerous guns.

On February 21, a TV news channel held a **town hall** in Sunrise, Florida. The topic of the meeting was gun policy. During the meeting, Cameron Kasky spoke with Florida senator Marco Rubio.

▲ Parkland student Cameron Kasky addresses Senator Marco Rubio (right) in Sunrise, Florida.

Cameron asked several times if Rubio would reject donations from the NRA. Rubio did not answer the question. Instead, he said he supported both school safety and the Second Amendment.

Next, Emma Gonzalez and NRA spokesperson Dana Loesch took the stage. Emma asked Loesch her opinion on semi-automatic guns and bump stocks. A bump stock allows a semi-automatic gun to fire dozens of bullets in seconds. In 2017, the shooter in Las Vegas used a bump stock. Emma wanted to make semi-automatics and bump stocks harder to buy. Loesch avoided answering Emma's question. Instead, she focused on mental health. Loesch said the NRA wanted to keep "insane" people from getting guns.

One month after the shooting, the Parkland students held a walkout. On March 14, most of the school's 3,000 students walked out of class. Students across the country did the same. They hoped to raise awareness of gun violence in schools.

Ten days later, Parkland students held the March for Our Lives protest in Washington, DC. The students had become well-known activists in a matter of weeks. Their protests had helped them gain support. However, the students also experienced opposition.

EMMA GONZALEZ

Emma Gonzalez's speech in Fort Lauderdale drew the attention of the nation. In her speech, Emma called out politicians for not doing enough. "Every single person up here today, all these people should be home grieving," Emma said. "But instead we are up here standing together because if all our government and president can do is send thoughts and prayers, then it's time for victims to be the change that we need to see."

Emma also spoke out about gun laws in Florida. "We certainly do not understand why it should be harder to make plans with friends on weekends than to buy an automatic or semi-automatic weapon." She explained that people did not need a permit or license to buy a gun in Florida. Buyers could purchase as many guns as they liked. And they did not need to **register** any of them.

▲ Emma Gonzalez has become the face of the Never Again movement.

Lastly, Emma called out politicians who accepted campaign donations from the NRA. "To every politician who is taking donations from the NRA, shame on you," Emma yelled. She asked the politicians whether they cared more about money than about human lives.

"Florida Student Emma Gonzalez to Lawmakers and Gun Advocates." *CNN*. CNN, 17 Feb. 2018. Web. 03 Sept. 2018.

CHAPTER 5

THE NRA RESPONDS

A week after the Parkland shooting, the NRA released a video. In the video, NRA TV host Colion Noir criticized the media. He said the media loved mass shootings. By covering shootings, news programs got higher ratings. Wayne LaPierre, the head of the NRA, also addressed the issue. He spoke out against those calling for more gun control. He argued that gun control supporters didn't even care about children.

NRA leader Wayne LaPierre is a strong supporter of gun rights.

Instead, they wanted to take away people's freedom.

LaPierre proposed a solution to school shootings. He argued for more armed security guards in schools. He repeated a line he had used after the 2012 shooting at Sandy Hook. He said good people with guns stop bad people with guns.

The NRA's solution to gun violence is to arm citizens. After the 2017 Las Vegas shooting, the NRA's Chris W. Cox pushed for fewer gun control laws. Cox said gun control does not increase safety. Instead, it leaves people defenseless. Cox called for a broader discussion about how to keep people safe. For example, he pointed to the film industry as one cause of gun violence. In his view, violent movies support irresponsible gun use.

In the month after the Parkland shooting, the NRA's Political Victory Fund raised $2.4 million.

▲ Protesters fight for gun rights at a rally in Pennsylvania in 2013.

This amount was the most the fund had raised in nearly 20 years. To achieve that result, the NRA had increased its online advertising. It also set a goal to gain 100,000 members in 100 days. To persuade people to join, the NRA claimed that gun rights were under more threat than ever.

▲ Students fight back against the NRA during the March for Our Lives protest in Washington, DC.

On the morning of the March for Our Lives protest, the NRA posted a message on Facebook. The post encouraged readers to join the NRA to fight for children's safety. It claimed people were taking advantage of children to **repeal** the Second Amendment.

Many people disagree with the NRA, including some gun owners. As of 2017, 30 percent of Americans owned guns. Most of those people own guns for personal protection. Others own them for hunting or for their jobs. Many owners support gun control in some form. In a 2018 survey, 78 percent of gun owners who were not NRA members supported background checks. Approximately 69 percent of NRA members were also supportive.

Other forms of gun control, such as a national firearms registry, had less support among gun owners. Many NRA members are against a gun registry. They do not want the government to track what they do.

Opinions about guns and gun control vary. Some gun owners support certain forms of gun control. And some people who don't own guns are against stricter laws. People on all sides want to reduce gun violence. However, they have different ideas of how to achieve that goal. These opposing ideas can make change slow to come.

CHAPTER 6

MAKING CHANGE

The Parkland students' efforts have helped bring change at the state level. On March 9, 2018, Florida's governor signed a school safety bill into law. This law has many features. It raises the minimum age to buy a rifle from 18 to 21. It also bans bump stocks. Under the new law, police officers can take guns away from people who are a threat to themselves or others. The law also includes $400 million to improve school safety.

Students in Alameda, California, participate in a walkout to protest gun violence in March 2018.

The funds will go toward school security, mental health services, and threat reporting.

Other states have also created new gun laws. Connecticut, Rhode Island, Vermont, and Washington have all banned bump stocks. Oregon made it illegal for people convicted of **stalking** or **domestic abuse** to buy guns. And in New York, people convicted of domestic abuse lose ownership of their guns.

New Jersey passed several gun laws in June 2018. One requires therapists to inform the police if a patient threatens serious violence. Another requires the state to file public reports on gun crimes. The reports show where guns that were used in crimes were obtained. Monthly police reports also list gun crimes in the state. They include the type of gun used, the place of the shooting, and the number of people shot.

▲ President Donald Trump meets with Parkland students to discuss school safety and gun violence.

Unlike some states and cities, the federal government has done little to change gun laws. President Trump supports the NRA's solution of putting more guns in schools. He has suggested arming guards and teachers. But Trump has also supported ideas that oppose the NRA's goals. For instance, he supported raising the minimum age to buy an AR-15 from 18 to 21.

A security officer greets students at a school in Connecticut.

Several US companies have joined the fight against gun violence. Bank of America stopped giving loans to businesses that make military-style guns for nonmilitary use. Another bank, Citigroup, put restrictions on clients that sell guns. These clients must ban bump stocks. They must also raise the minimum purchase age to 21. Walmart and L. L. Bean increased their minimum purchase age as well. And YouTube banned videos on how to make guns.

Other businesses have taken a different approach. In February 2018, nearly 20 companies said they would end their association with the NRA. Previously, Delta Air Lines had offered discounted tickets to NRA members. Avis, a car rental company, had offered lower rates to NRA members. MetLife, an insurance company, had also given lower rates. These companies stopped offering benefits to NRA members. In doing so, they took steps to reduce the NRA's influence.

THINK ABOUT IT ◄

Do you think teachers should be allowed to carry guns in schools? Why or why not?

CHAPTER 7

THE PARKLAND STUDENTS' LEGACY

Tragedies like the Parkland shooting give greater **urgency** to the gun control debate. However, as time passes, the need for change can feel less urgent. The Parkland students did not want this to happen. They continued to speak out against gun violence.

In June 2018, some Parkland students set out across the United States by bus. Their Road to Change tour was scheduled to last two months.

The March for Our Lives movement inspired people across the nation.

In June, they visited more than a dozen locations in the Midwest. In July, they made stops in Texas, California, and states in between. The students visited some cities to meet survivors of other mass shootings. They also visited cities where the NRA had given money to politicians. They wanted to make voters aware of the NRA's influence. Along the tour, the students helped young people register to vote. That way, more Americans could vote for candidates who opposed the NRA.

The Parkland students created a movement. Although they faced opponents, they also gained support. The March for Our Lives protest drew many first-time activists. It also attracted celebrities. Actor George Clooney and human rights lawyer Amal Clooney donated $500,000 to the protest. Oprah Winfrey donated the same amount.

Students take part in the March for Our Lives protest in Columbia, South Carolina, in March 2018.

The Parkland students continue to educate Americans about gun violence and gun control. And their movement shows no signs of stopping. In February 2018, the students faced death. They lost classmates, friends, and coaches. The experience changed them forever. By protesting, they hope to change their country forever.

FOCUS ON
PARKLAND STUDENTS

Write your answers on a separate piece of paper.

1. Write a paragraph describing the main ideas of Chapter 3.

2. Do you think creating stricter gun control laws will help reduce mass shootings? Why or why not?

3. What percentage of Americans reported owning a gun in 2017?

    A. 30 percent
    B. 48 percent
    C. 60 percent

4. Which measure do most Americans agree on?

    A. banning all guns
    B. requiring background checks
    C. banning semi-automatic guns

Answer key on page 48.

GLOSSARY

background checks
Reports on people's criminal, financial, and other history.

domestic abuse
Violence that someone commits against a person in his or her household.

lobbies
Tries to influence the decisions of politicians and other officials.

magazine
A device that holds ammunition to be fed into the chamber of a gun.

militia
A group of citizens with some military training.

ratified
Given official approval.

register
To make a record on an official list.

repeal
To cancel or reverse.

stalking
The crime of following others in a threatening, unwanted way.

town hall
A meeting where politicians answer questions from the audience.

traumatized
Experiencing lasting fear and shock after a difficult experience.

urgency
A need for immediate attention.

TO LEARN MORE

BOOKS

Hand, Carol. *Gun Control and the Second Amendment*. Minneapolis: Abdo Publishing, 2017.

Murray, Hallie. *The Right to Bear Arms: The Second Amendment*. New York: Enslow Publishing, 2018.

Orr, Tamra B. *Tucson Shooting and Gun Control*. Ann Arbor, MI: Cherry Lake Publishing, 2018.

NOTE TO EDUCATORS

Visit **www.focusreaders.com** to find lesson plans, activities, links, and other resources related to this title.

INDEX

Answer Key: 1. Answers will vary; **2.** Answers will vary; **3.** A; **4.** B